MAGELLAN
& THE EXPLORATION OF SOUTH AMERICA

BY

COLIN HYNSON

Europe

Africa

Antarctica

The above map shows the voyages of Ferdinand Magellan and Francisco Pizarro.

BARRON'S

Ferdinand Magellan

When Christopher Columbus sailed across the Atlantic in 1492 his intention was to discover a westward route to China and the East Indies. An eastward route was blocked to Europeans by hostile Muslim lands. Columbus never found Asia, but he did discover, after four voyages, a continent virtually unknown to Europeans—America. However, Columbus and others continued to believe that it was possible to journey westward and reach Asia by sailing around the American continent. It was this dream that inspired Ferdinand Magellan to sail away on a quest that would become the first voyage to circumnavigate the world. Magellan proved that it was possible to reach Asia by traveling to the west, but he paid for this discovery with his life—he was killed before the voyage was completed.

A WOODCUT PRINT OF MAGELLAN

Magellan was born in 1480 into a noble family in the Portuguese town of Sabrosa. He spent his early years as a page at the Portuguese royal court in Lisbon before joining the Portuguese navy.

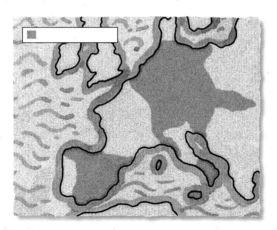

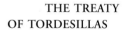

THE MOST POWERFUL MONARCH IN EUROPE

Charles V ruled over Spain, the Netherlands, Southern Italy, most of modern-day Germany and Austria and Spanish-conquered America and Africa, known as "the Holy Roman Empire." He provided the finance for Magellan's trip and continued to pay for the conquest and colonization of South and Central America.

THE TREATY OF TORDESILLAS

To prevent further rivalry between Spain and Portugal Pope Alexander VI issued the Treaty of Tordesillas in 1494. This gave Spain control over all non-Christian lands west of an imaginary line in the mid Atlantic. Portugal was given everything to the east.

THE RISE OF PORTUGAL

This engraving of Lisbon in the 1550s shows that Portugal was an important and wealthy seafaring and trading nation. Portugal had successfully freed itself from Muslim rule by 1250 and turned its attention to the exploration of the Atlantic coast of West Africa. The Portuguese discovery of a route around Africa to Asia meant that they controlled the spice trade to Europe. It was for this reason that Spain financed Magellan's trip to find an alternative route to the East.

MAGELLAN TAKES TO THE SEA

While Magellan served with the Portuguese navy he traveled to many parts of the world, including India and West Africa. He took part in battles against the Arabs on the Indian Ocean. Afterward he fought against the Moors in North Africa, where he was injured. He asked the king of Portugal, Manuel I, for an increase in his pension. Manuel replied by dismissing him and Magellan offered his services to Charles V.

FERDINAND MAGELLAN
-A Time Line-

~1476~
Francisco Pizarro born.

~1480~
Ferdinand Magellan born.

~1485~
Hernando Cortes born.

~1494~
Treaty of Tordesillas between Spain and Portugal signed dividing the non-Christian world between them.

~1500~
Brazil discovered by Pedro Alvarez Cabral.

~1502~
Pizarro sails for Hispaniola.

Montezuma ascends the throne of the Aztec empire.

~1504~
Cortes sails for Hispaniola.

KING JOHN II OF PORTUGAL

John II ruled Portugal from 1481 to 1495. He had been placed in charge of Portuguese explorations by his father in 1474, and he encouraged the exploration of the African coast and the Middle East. Columbus had asked him for money to finance his trip across the Atlantic, but John turned him down. In 1492 he admitted thousands of wealthy Jews into Portugal after they had been expelled by Spain, only to expel them a few years later in 1497–8.

Preparing for the Voyage

*I*t took only two months for Magellan to convince the Spanish king, Charles I (who became the Holy Roman Emperor Charles V in 1519), to finance his voyage to discover a westward route to Asia from the west. Charles I allowed Magellan to be commander of the fleet and to keep five percent of any profit made from the trip. Magellan took a close interest in how his ships were equipped and records still exist which show exactly what Magellan took on his voyage. These include details of weapons, navigational instruments, food, and goods for trade. He had five ships: the *San Antonio,* the *Trinidad,* the *Concepción,* the *Santiago,* and the *Victoria.* The crews totaled over 230 and were of many different nationalities, including French, Portuguese, Italian, African, and Malaysian. Magellan was the only non-Spanish officer.

MAGELLAN'S SHIPS

Of the five ships in Magellan's fleet, four, including the *Victoria* pictured here, were carracks. Carracks were large vessels that were originally built to be merchant ships. On expeditions they carried supplies and most of the weapons. The *Santiago* was a caravel. Caravels were much smaller and lighter, with triangular sails that made them better for navigating in coastal waters. Carracks had three masts or more while the typical caravel had only two.

THE SUPPORT OF THE KING

Charles I approved Magellan's plan and agreed to pay for the voyage in September 1518. It took Magellan one year to gather together a crew and prepare his ships at the Spanish port of Sanlúcar in Seville. It is likely that Magellan had no intention of sailing around the world and was planning to return by the same route that he was to take from Spain.

A HUNTING FALCON

Magellan knew that if his trip was to be successful he had to trade with people he met on his voyage. He took many things to barter with, such as printed handkerchiefs, scissors, knives, glass beads, and about 20,000 bells that could be attached to the feet of trained hunting birds. European explorers had found that many people in both America and Africa found hawkbells fascinating.

THE QUADRANT

Along with astrolabes, Magellan took twenty-one quadrants, which measured the angle between the horizon and the sun or stars and which gave the user his latitude position. Magellan also took a set of tables which showed the position of the sun at different latitudes to enable him to calculate his position more accurately.

FERDINAND MAGELLAN
-A TIME LINE-

~1505~
*Magellan joins the
Portuguese navy.*

~1506~
*Magellan sails to
the East Indies.*

~1511~
*Cuba conquered by
Diego de Velazquez de Cuélla.*

~1513~
*Magellan is injured while
fighting in North Africa.*

*Vasco Nunez de Balboa is
the first European to see
the Pacific Ocean.*

*Juan Ponce de Leon
discovers Florida.*

~1514~
*The colony of
Panama established.*

~1518~
*After a quarrel with
King Manuel I of Portugal,
Magellan begins to work for
Charles I of Spain. Charles V
agrees to fund Magellan's
voyage to find Asia.*

THE ASTROLABE

Magellan took seven astrolabes on his voyage. Astrolabes could find the latitude of a ship by measuring the height of the North Star or the noon sun. The above picture is a land-based Astrolabe, though the principles are the same for both.

WEAPONS ON BOARD

Magellan knew that the voyage he was about to take was vulnerable to attack. He prepared for this by taking a large amount of weapons, including 1,000 lances, 60 crossbows, and 120 spears. He also had cannons similar to these although cannons on board ship did not have wheels at this time.

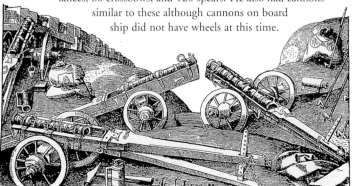

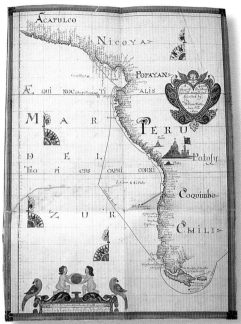

LANDING AT RIO DE JANEIRO

Three months after setting sail from Spain, Magellan reached the Brazilian coast on December 6, 1519. Magellan was nervous because the whole area was controlled by Portugal. He sailed south until he landed at present-day Rio de Janeiro. After stocking up with fresh supplies the ships continued south and spent that winter at San Julián in Patagonia.

THE SPANISH CAPTAINS MUTINY

After spending the winter at San Julián, Magellan invited all the captains to eat with him. None of them came and instead they sent a demand that the fleet return to Spain. Magellan acted ruthlessly. The captain of the *Victoria* was killed and others were either imprisoned or abandoned on the shore. In October 1520, as they neared the South Pole, the captain and crew of the *San Antonio* mutinied again and sailed back toward Spain.

AROUND THE TIP OF SOUTH AMERICA

On October 21, 1520, the ships entered what is today known as the *Magellan Strait,* although Magellan himself called it Canal de Todos los Santos (All Saints' Channel). The strait was a narrow and dangerous channel and they were sailing straight into the wind. Sometimes the wind was so strong the ships had to be towed by rowing boats. It took them thirty-eight days to sail through the strait. With only three ships left Magellan eventually reached the Pacific Ocean on November 28, 1520.

SIGHTING STRANGE ANIMALS

Magellan and his men had sailed further south than any other European and they saw many different creatures. They caught animals such as seals and penguins for food. Pigafetta called the seals *"sea wolves"* and he thought the penguins were geese. In his diary he said, *"These geese are black...and they do not fly, and live upon fish. They have beaks like that of a crow."*

Setting Off

The five ships sailed from Sanlúcar on September 20, 1519, with the *Trinidad* leading the way. An Italian nobleman, Antonio Pigafetta, kept diaries for the whole of the journey. From these diaries it is clear that Magellan faced many difficulties on board ship. The other officers on the voyage disliked Magellan because he was Portuguese and they plotted against him. He had to deal with several mutinies during his voyage. At first he had to treat the crew with care. According to Pigafetta, he did not tell them where they were going *"so that his men should not from amazement and fear be unwilling to accompany him on so long a voyage."* After stopping for supplies at the Canary Islands, Magellan sailed along the West African coast in order to avoid Portuguese patrol ships before setting off across the Atlantic.

ST. ELMO'S FIRE

The ships hit a massive Atlantic storm. The electrical charge created huge sparks that made the ships' masts appear to be on fire. The crew thought the lights were saints protecting them and called them St. Elmo's Fire.

SEARCHING FOR THE STRAIT

While sailing along the South American coast Magellan sent ships ahead to search for the route around South America. He explored the entrance to the River Plate thinking it might be the entrance to the Pacific. The *Santiago* was sunk while searching for the strait, causing even more resentment among his crew.

The Voyage Completed

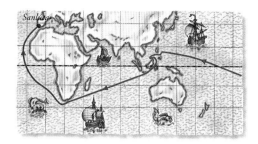

Magellan reached the Pacific Ocean more than one year after leaving Spain. He had put down two mutinies, lost one ship to a rebellious crew with another wrecked. When the three remaining ships left the strait they became the first Europeans to sail into the Pacific Ocean. But they were not the first Europeans to see the Pacific Ocean. Vasco de Balboa had this honor. He crossed Central America to the west coast by foot in 1513. Balboa had simply named the ocean the *"Great South Sea."* Magellan named it the Pacific Ocean because of the gentle winds he found there. Many of his crew wanted to return home, but Magellan believed that it was now only a short journey to Asia. They sailed for three more months, seeing only two uninhabited islands (which they named the Unfortunate Islands) before finally landing at Guam.

THE VAST OCEAN

The three-month journey accross the ocean took its toll on the crew. Their biscuits had either been eaten by rats or were rotten. The water was too foul for many to drink. The crew were so desperate that they ate sawdust, rats, and strips of leather. Many became very ill with scurvy and twenty-nine died.

THE DEATH OF MAGELLAN

Cilapulapu, one of the islands of the Philippines, refused to accept Spanish rule. On April 27, 1521, Magellan and sixty armed men tried to subdue Cilapulapu. In the battle that followed, Magellan was hit by a spear and was then hacked to death.

ARRIVAL AT THE PHILIPPINES

It took another week for the fleet to sail from Guam and arrive at the Philippines. Here sick sailors were put ashore to recover and Magellan began trading with the local inhabitants. In exchange for some of the hawkbells and mirrors Magellan had brought with him, he was given a basket of ginger and a bar of gold.

MONUMENT TO MAGELLAN AT CEBU

When Magellan reached the island of Cebu after leaving the Philippines, he calculated that he was now west of the Spice Islands, which had already been visited by Europeans traveling eastward. It was at this point that he knew it was possible to sail around the world.

LANDING AT GUAM

On March 6, 1521, Magellan reached the island of Guam, part of the modern Marianas Islands. There was obvious relief at reaching land and the opportunity to stock up with fresh supplies. The local people pictured here tried to steal one of their landing boats. Magellan reacted by calling the islands Ladrones, or Thieves, Islands. He also burned down a village to set an example.

FERDINAND MAGELLAN
-A Time Line-

~1519~
Panama City founded.

Magellan's ships sail away from Spain.

Cortes and his army enter Tenochtitlan.

~December 6, 1519~
Magellan arrives at the South American coast and then sails on to Rio de Janiero.

~1520~
Magellan reaches San Julian in Argentina and spends the winter there.

Magellan deals with the mutiny by his Spanish captains.

The Aztecs drive Cortes out of Tenochtitlan.

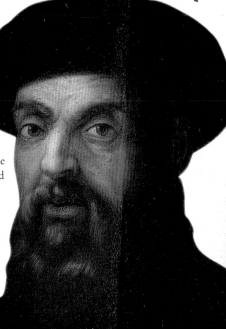

TIERRA DEL FUEGO

Sailing through the Magellan Straits at night they saw many fires from distant Indian camps. They then called the land Tierra del Fuego, the *"Land of Fires."* Once through, the ships remained close while sailing up the west coast of South America.

THE JOURNEY HOME

When Magellan was killed, the *Trinidad* and the *Victoria* headed back to Spain. Only the *Victoria* completed the journey home. The voyage had brought no profit to the Spanish king, but Magellan had proved that a westward route to Asia did exist.

Hernando Cortes & the Aztecs

The Spanish conquered Cuba in 1511 under the command of Diego de Velazquez. From here they set out in ships to search for gold on the central American mainland. In 1517 Francisco de Cordoba sailed to Yucatan on the mainland where he met the Mayan people, but they quickly drove him away. Another expedition a year later was more successful, and they brought back gold to Cuba. In 1519 Velazquez ordered Hernando Cortes, who had helped in the conquest of Cuba, to lead an expedition to explore the interior of Mexico. An argument between the two men led to Cortes renouncing Velazquez and setting off with his own private army. Little did Cortes realize that he would encounter a great empire and one of the largest cities in the known world and that with only a few hundred soldiers he would destroy both.

HERNANDO CORTES

Hernando Cortes was born in 1485 into a Spanish noble family. He studied for two years at the University of Salamanca. In 1504 he arrived in the New World and fought in the conquest of Cuba in 1511.

MARINA THE TRANSLATOR

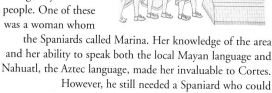

Soon after he landed in Yucatan, Cortes was given slaves as a gift by the local people. One of these was a woman whom the Spaniards called Marina. Her knowledge of the area and her ability to speak both the local Mayan language and Nahuatl, the Aztec language, made her invaluable to Cortes. However, he still needed a Spaniard who could speak Mayan in order to talk to the Aztecs.

MOUNT POPOCATEPETL

On their way to the Aztec capital, the Spaniards passed the volcano Mount Popocatepetl. It was belching smoke. They had never seen a live volcano before and Cortes sent some men up the mountain to see where the smoke was coming from. They were forced back by the hot ash.

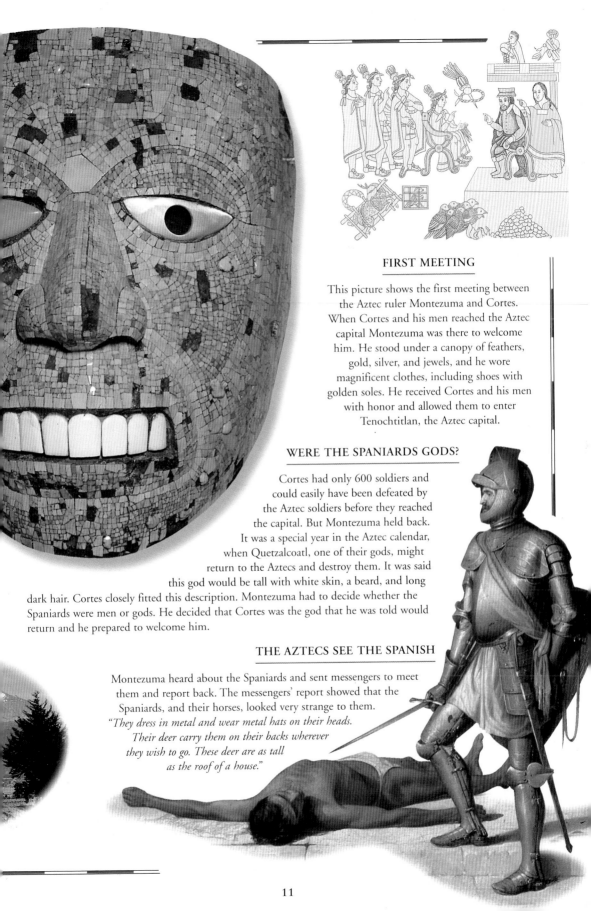

FIRST MEETING

This picture shows the first meeting between the Aztec ruler Montezuma and Cortes. When Cortes and his men reached the Aztec capital Montezuma was there to welcome him. He stood under a canopy of feathers, gold, silver, and jewels, and he wore magnificent clothes, including shoes with golden soles. He received Cortes and his men with honor and allowed them to enter Tenochtitlan, the Aztec capital.

WERE THE SPANIARDS GODS?

Cortes had only 600 soldiers and could easily have been defeated by the Aztec soldiers before they reached the capital. But Montezuma held back. It was a special year in the Aztec calendar, when Quetzalcoatl, one of their gods, might return to the Aztecs and destroy them. It was said this god would be tall with white skin, a beard, and long dark hair. Cortes closely fitted this description. Montezuma had to decide whether the Spaniards were men or gods. He decided that Cortes was the god that he was told would return and he prepared to welcome him.

THE AZTECS SEE THE SPANISH

Montezuma heard about the Spaniards and sent messengers to meet them and report back. The messengers' report showed that the Spaniards, and their horses, looked very strange to them.
"They dress in metal and wear metal hats on their heads. Their deer carry them on their backs wherever they wish to go. These deer are as tall as the roof of a house."

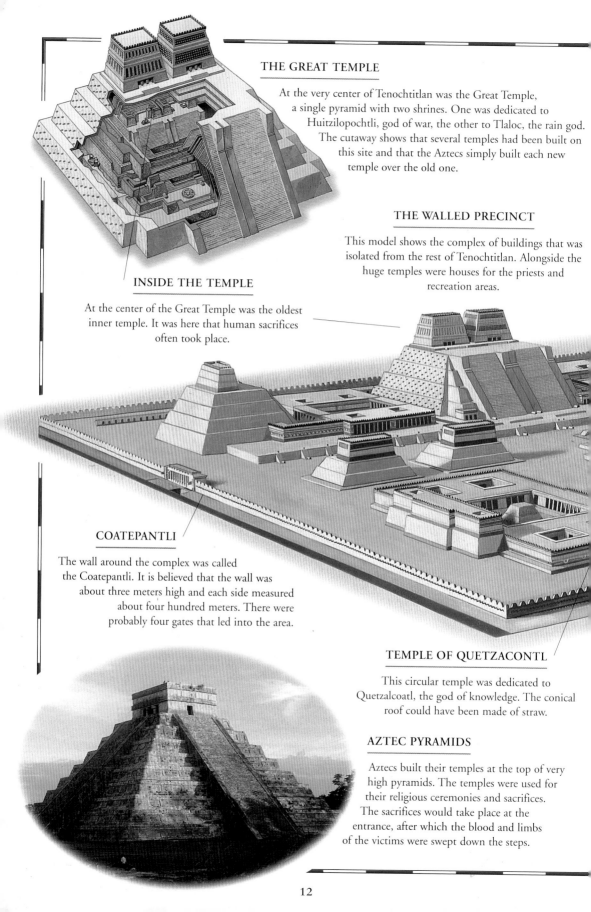

THE GREAT TEMPLE

At the very center of Tenochtitlan was the Great Temple,
a single pyramid with two shrines. One was dedicated to
Huitzilopochtli, god of war, the other to Tlaloc, the rain god.
The cutaway shows that several temples had been built on
this site and that the Aztecs simply built each new
temple over the old one.

THE WALLED PRECINCT

This model shows the complex of buildings that was
isolated from the rest of Tenochtitlan. Alongside the
huge temples were houses for the priests and
recreation areas.

INSIDE THE TEMPLE

At the center of the Great Temple was the oldest
inner temple. It was here that human sacrifices
often took place.

COATEPANTLI

The wall around the complex was called
the Coatepantli. It is believed that the wall was
about three meters high and each side measured
about four hundred meters. There were
probably four gates that led into the area.

TEMPLE OF QUETZACONTL

This circular temple was dedicated to
Quetzalcoatl, the god of knowledge. The conical
roof could have been made of straw.

AZTEC PYRAMIDS

Aztecs built their temples at the top of very
high pyramids. The temples were used for
their religious ceremonies and sacrifices.
The sacrifices would take place at the
entrance, after which the blood and limbs
of the victims were swept down the steps.

The Aztec Empire

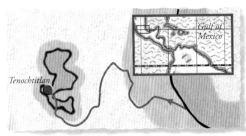

Cortes's journey to Tenochtitlan, 1519

When Cortes and his men arrived at Tenochtitlan they had reached the center of a huge empire which stretched from the Atlantic to the Pacific coast. The Aztecs were a wandering tribe until they began to build the city of Tenochtitlan around a temple to one of their gods, Huitzilopochtli, around the year 1300. They built the city on a series of islands on Lake Texcoco. The city had aqueducts, canals, and a huge causeway linking it to the mainland. By the 1500s it had a population of about 300,000 and was larger than any European city. The wealth of the Aztecs came from conquered peoples who had to pay tribute to them.

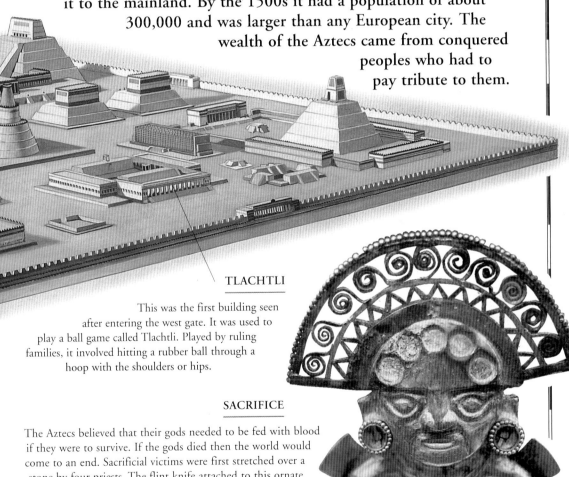

TLACHTLI

This was the first building seen after entering the west gate. It was used to play a ball game called Tlachtli. Played by ruling families, it involved hitting a rubber ball through a hoop with the shoulders or hips.

SACRIFICE

The Aztecs believed that their gods needed to be fed with blood if they were to survive. If the gods died then the world would come to an end. Sacrificial victims were first stretched over a stone by four priests. The flint knife attached to this ornate hilt would have been used by a fifth priest to cut open the victim's chest and his still beating heart removed and placed in a bowl. The arms and legs of the victim were also eaten. Most of the victims were prisoners captured in battles.

The Aztec Empire

As the Spanish advanced through the Aztec empire and entered Tenochtitlan, they encountered a civilization that must have seemed to them to be both very cruel and yet very advanced. The Aztecs had a huge and fantastically wealthy empire of at least 12 million people, advanced agriculture, a magnificent city with beautiful palaces, a zoo, and colorful gardens. They were the most powerful people in Central America. One of Cortes's soldiers, Bernal Diaz, later wrote of his encounter with the Aztecs: *"With such wonderful sights to gaze on we did not know what to say, or if what we saw was real."* Their calendars, ways of writing, and the gods they worshiped may have sounded strange to the Spaniards, but Aztec life was as sophisticated as anything that would have been found in other parts of the known world.

A MULTITUDE OF GODS

The Aztecs believed in many gods and goddesses. Each of them looked after an aspect of Aztec life. There were four important gods. Tlaloc was the god of rain and storms. Tezcatlipoca was the god of darkness and evil. Huitzilopochtli was the god of light and war. Quetzalcoatl was the god of life. The Aztec priests were very powerful people.

POLE CEREMONY

Aztec religion demanded many different ceremonies and rituals. In one of these, men would use feathers to dress themselves as birds and would then be attached to ropes and swung around in a wide circle. As the photograph shows, this practice is still continued in modern Mexico.

PLAYING PATOLLI

Along with ball games such as Tlachtli, the Aztecs also played board games like Patolli. The board was in four sections and divided into 52 parts, symbolizing the 52 years of the Aztec century. The game involved throwing dice and differently colored beans until one player had three beans in a row. This and other games were often of religious significance and would have dire consequences—the loser and his family could become slaves. In Tlachtli players were often badly injured and the loser might be sacrificed.

AZTEC CALENDAR STONE

This large stone, one of the largest Aztec sculptures found, shows their belief that the world has been through four stages that have been created and destroyed. The Aztecs believed they were living in the fifth age, which would be destroyed by a massive earthquake. The human race and the sun and the moon were created at the start of the fifth world. At the center of the stone is the face of the sun.

WRITING AND READING

The Aztecs did not use letters for writing words. They had a kind of picture-writing system called glyphs (an example is shown left) where every object was represented as a drawing. There were strict rules about how these drawings were created. Aztec books were called codices. They were made out of bark and the pages were joined together to make one long book.

COAST NEAR CEMPOALLA

The Aztecs were wealthy because the people they conquered had to pay tribute to them. When the Aztecs took over new lands they allowed the people living there to continue following their own lives as long as they sent a tribute every year. This tribute was usually locally produced food. On the coast of Cempoalla this would have been fish.

THE DEATH OF MONTEZUMA

When Cortes first left the city fighting had broken out between the Aztecs and the Spanish. The Aztec leaders decided to depose the imprisoned Montezuma and replace him with his brother Cuitlahuac. Cortes did not realize that Montezuma was no longer seen as the ruler of the Aztecs, and he brought him to the roof of the royal palace to appeal to his people. They replied by throwing stones at him and attacking the palace. One of the stones hit Montezuma and he was later found dead. Both sides accused the other of killing him. His body was taken away and thrown into one of the nearby canals.

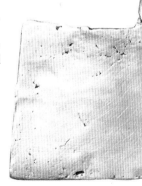

FERDINAND MAGELLAN
-A Time Line-

~1520~
The strait between the Atlantic and Pacific is sighted, and after several months Magellan emerges into the Pacific.

~1521~
Magellan lands at Guam/Ladrones Islands, followed by the Philippines where he is killed.

Fighting between Aztecs and Spaniards starts.

Cortes returns to Tenochtitlan with a new army and the Aztecs finally surrender.

THE SIEGE BEGINS

Along with his new army Cortes also had built twelve or thirteen ships which he armed with cannons from Cuba. These he used on the lake that surrounded the island city of Tenochtitlan to bombard the Aztec defenders. The Aztecs found themselves attacked from both inside and outside their city. Starving and weak with disease, the Aztecs held out against the Spanish and their allies for several months.

SMALLPOX IN THE CITY

In the end it was not Spanish weapons that defeated the Aztecs. An outbreak of smallpox, a disease brought over from Europe, spread throughout the city and many people died even before the siege began.

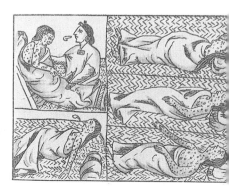

The Destruction of the Aztecs

fter several days in Tenochtitlan Cortes and his small army began to worry for their safety. They had seen the blood-stained steps of the Aztec temples and thought that the Aztecs were devil worshipers. They felt that it was only Montezuma who stopped the Aztecs from killing them all. Cortes decided to take Montezuma prisoner and to use him to rule the Aztecs. Montezuma must by then have realized that these men were not gods. Cortes stayed for several months before leaving to deal with a rival expedition from Cuba.

THE EMPIRE DESTROYED

Cuahtemoc, the nephew of Montezuma, became the new Aztec ruler and had to face Cortes's attack. He held out for four months fighting on the streets of Tenochtitlan before finally surrendering in August 1521. He was tortured and hanged.

AZTEC GOLD

The Aztecs believed they could appease the Spanish by giving them vast amounts of gold. Montezuma took them to the treasure house where, according to one Aztec, *"The Spaniards stripped the feathers from the golden shields. They put all the gold in one large pile and set fire to everything else, even if it was valuable. They then melted the gold and turned it into bars."*

CORTES RETURNS

It was while Cortes was away that the Spaniards attacked the Aztecs. Cortes returned and tried to use Montezuma to calm the Aztecs, but the royal palace was besieged and he had to fight his way out of Tenochtitlan. In May 1521 he came back with an army of 100,000 local people who hated the Aztecs. He cut off all supplies of food and water to the city before launching his final attack.

The Inca Empire

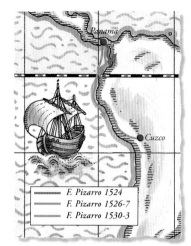

n what is now part of modern Peru, Ecuador, Argentina, Chile, and Bolivia rose the Andean empire of the Incas, which was even larger than the Aztec empire. The empire expanded in the 14th century (from what is now Ayacucho in Peru) under the leadership of Pachacutec. According to accounts given to the Spanish, most of the Inca empire was created under his rule. By the time the Incas came into conflict with the Spanish, they controlled a population of about 12 million people and an empire that stretched 4,000 kilometers from south to north. This is remarkable given that the Incas did not possess horses or wheeled vehicles.

MODERN ANDEAN WOMAN

The legacy of the Incas still lives on. Even though the ancestors of the people of the Andean lands had been subjected to conquest, colonization, and Spanish rule, many aspects of Inca life are still in evidence today. The Incas would have recognized the way that these people still farm and fish. The clothes worn by this woman have changed little in style.

INCA GODS

Like the Aztecs, the Incas worshiped many gods. The most important god was Viracocha. He emerged from Lake Titicaca and then created the first men from clay. Under him were gods of the earth, the sea, storms, the sun, the moon, and the stars. Every season there were celebrations for different gods. Inti, the sun god, was particularly important as the Inca rulers believed that they were descended from him. At Cuzco a temple dedicated to Inti had doors that were entirely covered in gold.

THE CITY OF CUZCO

The city shown in the adjacent picture is Cuzco, the capital city of the Incas. It was designed in the form of a puma, because the puma represented strength and power to the Incas. A fortress at one end was the head and two rivers were straightened out to form the tail. The buildings were made of massive stone blocks that fitted together so well that no mortar was needed to hold them together.

FERDINAND MAGELLAN
-A Time Line-

~1522~
Magellan's ship Victoria *arrives back in Spain.*

~1523~
Guatemala conquered and settled by Pedro de Alvarado.

~1524~
Cortes leads an expedition to Honduras.

The colony of Nicaragua established.

INCA TECHNOLOGY

These three pictures show how advanced Inca technology was. The picture on the far left shows the rope bridges that the Incas built to link their 20,000 kms. of paved roads. The center picture shows how they used lengths of string called quipos to keep count. The one on the right shows some of the sophisticated methods used in their agriculture.

ATAHUALPA SEIZED

The Spaniards used the same methods to subdue the Incas as they used against the Aztecs. The Inca ruler, Atahualpa, had invited the Spaniards into his kingdom and met them at the town of Cajamarca. He was handed a Bible which he threw away. The Spanish soldiers then captured him and attacked Atahualpa's followers.

ATAHUALPA AS A PRISONER

A Spaniard called Francisco de Xeres wrote a book about the conquest of the Incas in 1534. According to him the Spanish commander, Francisco Pizarro, *"presently ordered native clothes to be brought, and when Atabaliba was dressed, he made him sit near him, and soothed his rage and agitation at finding himself so quickly fallen from his high estate."*

The Inca Empire

One of the most spectacular monuments of the Inca empire is the ruined town of Machu Picchu. It lay undiscovered until it was found by an American archaeologist, Hiram Bingham, in 1911. It was never discovered by the Spanish invaders, so they did not have the chance to destroy it. It might have been a frontier outpost and was probably dedicated to Inti, the sun god.

MACHU PICCHU

Machu Picchu is about 80 km. northwest of Cuzco and is nearly 2,400 meters above sea level.

ATHABALIBA
ultimus Rex Peruanorum.

The Destruction of the Inca Empire

The Spaniards in Central America heard rumors of a land in the south called Biru, or Peru, that was filled with gold and other precious metals. Francisco Pizarro decided to sail down the coast from the town of Panama, which the Spaniards had built in 1519. He led an expedition in 1527 and discovered the city of Tumbez. They were welcomed by the inhabitants and shown much gold and silver. Pizarro was now convinced he had found a huge source of gold and he returned to Spain. Charles V gave him permission to conquer this new land and made him Governor and Captain General of Peru. He returned in 1530 with an army of about 180 soldiers.

CIVIL WAR

Pizarro was certainly helped by the fact that the Incas were fighting a civil war. Inca rulers were called the Sapa Inca. In 1527 the Sapa Inca, Huayna Capac, died of smallpox. He had two sons, Huascar and Atahualpa, who both claimed his title. The final battle was fought as Pizarro approached and Huascar had been taken prisoner.

DEMAND FOR GOLD

After he was taken prisoner himself, Atahualpa thought that if he gave the Spaniards enough gold to fill a large room they would let him go. Pizarro agreed to release him and Atahualpa ordered gold to be stripped from temples and palaces. Over 7 tons of gold were collected and melted down.

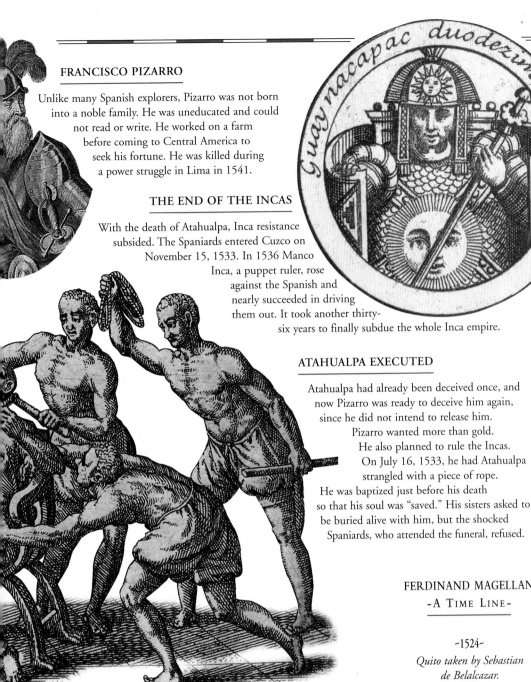

FRANCISCO PIZARRO

Unlike many Spanish explorers, Pizarro was not born into a noble family. He was uneducated and could not read or write. He worked on a farm before coming to Central America to seek his fortune. He was killed during a power struggle in Lima in 1541.

THE END OF THE INCAS

With the death of Atahualpa, Inca resistance subsided. The Spaniards entered Cuzco on November 15, 1533. In 1536 Manco Inca, a puppet ruler, rose against the Spanish and nearly succeeded in driving them out. It took another thirty-six years to finally subdue the whole Inca empire.

ATAHUALPA EXECUTED

Atahualpa had already been deceived once, and now Pizarro was ready to deceive him again, since he did not intend to release him. Pizarro wanted more than gold. He also planned to rule the Incas. On July 16, 1533, he had Atahualpa strangled with a piece of rope. He was baptized just before his death so that his soul was "saved." His sisters asked to be buried alive with him, but the shocked Spaniards, who attended the funeral, refused.

FERDINAND MAGELLAN
-A TIME LINE-

~1524~
Quito taken by Sebastian de Belalcazar.

~1532~
Atahualpa seized by Pizarro.

~1533~
Atahualpa executed and Cuzco finally taken.

Ecuador conquered by Sebastian de Belalcazar.

PIZARRO AND ATAHUALPA MEET

Atahualpa was certainly confident after defeating his brother and he was curious to meet Pizarro. Although he took 3,000 soldiers with him to the meeting, he agreed that they would be unarmed after Pizarro said that he would not be harmed. The Spanish soldiers, although they were vastly outnumbered, brought their muskets and cannons with them. When Atahualpa was captured, hundreds of his soldiers were killed trying to defend him with no weapons.

EUROPEAN DISEASES

One of the main reasons for the terrible drop in population was the introduction of diseases such as smallpox and measles into the American continent. The people of South and Central America had no resistance to these new diseases and many died as a result.

BECOMING EUROPEAN

The Spanish and Portuguese conquerors felt that their way of life and Christianity were better than those of the people they had conquered. This picture shows that people were forced out of their native clothes and made to wear European fashions. It was hoped this would make them more European.

SURVIVING CUSTOMS

The Europeans did not succeed in completely destroying the cultures they came across. This mask shows that modern Mexicans still celebrate the *"Day of the Dead,"* which has its origins with the Aztecs. Even today, many people in South and Central America add bits of their old religions to their Christian worship.

DESTROYING IDOLS

The priests who traveled with the explorers were determined that the conquered people would become Christian. Many of these people felt that they had been defeated by a superior god and readily converted. The priests also stamped out all signs of the old religions by pulling down the temples and smashing the statues of gods. They replaced them with crosses and statues of the Virgin Mary.

Life in Spanish America

The arrival of the Spanish and the Portuguese in South and Central America had a devastating effect upon the people who were living there. In only a few years huge empires were destroyed by small groups of determined and cruel men driven by greed, personal ambition and religious zeal. These new rulers did not respect the ideas and customs of their new subjects. All over the conquered empires the Spaniards and Portuguese looted and destroyed. The population of Mexico was estimated to be 25 million in 1519. Due to disease and murder that figure had plummeted to nearly 2 million by 1580.

INDEPENDENCE

It was only in the first part of the 19th century that South and Central America finally broke away from their European rulers. It was the revolutionary Simon Bolivar who led many countries toward independence. Paraguay became independent in 1813, followed by Argentina in 1816. Chile became independent in 1818, followed by Mexico and Peru in 1821.

NEW BUILDINGS

Once the Spaniards had destroyed the temples and buildings they came across, they began to build on top of the ruins. Churches, such as this one in Cuzco, were built on the sites of old temples. Mexico City was built on the remains of Tenochtitlan using the stones from the dismantled buildings.

HARSH PUNISHMENTS

As more and more people from Spain came over to Mexico and South America, conditions for the conquered people continued to get worse. Thousands were enslaved and made to work in gold and silver mines where they suffered from terrible conditions and from overwork. This meant that their fields were left untended and many more went hungry. Anyone who disobeyed the Spanish was dealt with severely. This picture shows people being burned alive by their Spanish master.

The Impact of South America on Europe

From the ruined palaces of ancient empires through to the magnificent churches built by the Spanish and Portuguese, it is clear even today that the arrival of Europeans on American shores had a huge and devastating impact. Although it is more difficult to see the influence that South and Central America had on the lives of Europeans, they nevertheless had a similar impact. The most obvious was the huge amount of gold and silver that was taken to Spain. The Spanish king claimed one fifth of all gold and silver that was mined. This made Spain one of the wealthiest and most powerful nations in Europe. It is still possible to see Spanish churches decorated with gold that came from their conquered lands. Much of the food that we all take for granted was first grown in these lands.

NUTS AND BEANS

Many foods, such as peanuts, sweet potatoes, and kidney beans, originally came from South and Central America. They are now grown all over the world. Peanuts (above) are native to South America. They were first introduced to Africa by European explorers and then reached North America with the slave trade.

They are now cultivated all over the world, from India to Nigeria and the United States.

Sweet potatoes are native to Central America and were also found in the Andes. They were an important part of the Aztec diet and were taken to Europe in the 16th century and then later spread to Asia.

A Sta Prinsipal con sume esclava
Arbol de Granadillas, y su Frut
Arbol del Mispero, y su Fr
fruta con nombre de N
Palma de Cocos gran
Arbol de Coquitos de

Vicente Albean pintor
Quion a. 1783.

SQUASHES

Squashes such as pumpkins and courgettes were central to the diets of people in Central America. There is some evidence that they were beginning to be eaten by Indians in North America before the fifteenth century. However, it was the arrival of the Spanish explorers that speeded up the spread of squashes. They are now grown and eaten all over the world, particularly in Mediterranean countries and North America.

RUBBER AND MAHOGANY

Rubber was used by the peoples of America for centuries. Christopher Columbus observed the inhabitants of Haiti using rubber to make balls for games. The Aztecs used rubber balls to play Tlachtli. But it was not until the start of the 19th century, when a way was found to keep rubber soft when it became solid, that it began to be used commercially. Mahogany has been used for making fine furniture since 1500. European demand for mahogany led to many South American forests being cleared. Their continued destruction is a major concern for modern environmentalists.

FERDINAND MAGELLAN
-A TIME LINE-

~1535~
Lima founded by Pizarro.

~1537~
*The Chibchas of Columbia
are conquered by
Gonzalo Jimenez de Quesada.*

~1540~
Cortes returns to Spain.

~1541~
Pizarro assassinated.

*Mississippi discovered by
Hernando de Soto.*

~1542~
*Orellana reaches the mouth
of the Amazon.*

~1547~
Cortes dies near Seville.

CORN

Along with the sweet potato, corn was the most important crop of both South and Central America. The Aztecs ground corn into flour, which was then turned into tortillas or tamales and stuffed with vegetables or atolli, a kind of porridge. The Incas also used corn to make a porridge called capia. The United States now grows nearly half of all the world's corn.

Other Explorers of South America

PEDRO DE ALVARADO

Alvarado was second in command to Cortes during the conquest of the Aztecs. After Tenochtitlan was destroyed and Mexico City built, he became its first mayor. In 1523 he conquered and settled Guatemala, and he later assisted in the conquest of Honduras.

Although the Spanish explorers had a reputation for being bloodthirsty and cruel, it must be remembered that they conquered the great civilizations of the Aztecs and Incas with only a few hundred soldiers. This must have taken a lot of courage, daring, and a certain amount of good luck. Pizarro and Cortes were not the only explorers of South and Central America. Many more men set out into unexplored areas with little idea of the dangers that lay ahead of them.

JUAN PONCE DE LEON

De Leon was born in 1460 and sailed with Columbus in 1493. He spent most of his time either in Cuba or fighting in Puerto Rico. While he was in Cuba he heard rumors of an island that had the fabled Fountain of Youth. He set sail to find the fountain, but instead he landed at Florida, his most famous discovery.

PEDRO ARIAS DAVILA

Davila established Spanish colonies in Panama in 1514 and Nicaragua in 1524. He also founded Panama City in 1519. It was Davila who first sent Pizarro to conquer the Incas. He became governor of Nicaragua in 1526, where he stayed until his death in 1531.

PEDRO ALVAREZ CABRAL

Cabral discovered Brazil almost by accident. In 1500 he had been sent by the king of Portugal to sail to India along the African coast. Soon after he set off he was blown too far west and he reached land which he named *"Island of the True Cross."* It was later called Brazil. He then set sail for India but on the way lost five of the thirteen ships pictured here.

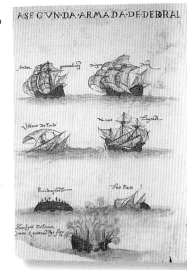

VASCO NUNEZ DE BALBOA

Balboa was an adventurer who stowed away on a ship heading from Hispaniola in the Caribbean to San Sebastian in Central America. He convinced the people there to resettle and then made himself their leader. He heard rumors of a huge sea and, with only a few hundred men, set off across Panama to find it. He was the first European to see the Pacific Ocean which he claimed for Spain.

HERNANDO DE ALARCON

Alarcon commanded two ships that supported an overland expedition in 1540 from Mexico into the region now known as the southwestern United States. Alarcon sailed to the head of the Gulf of California and proved that there was no water passage between the Gulf and the Pacific. He was also one of the first Europeans to sail along the Colorado River.

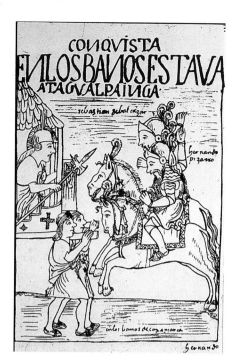

SEBASTIAN DE BELALCAZAR

Belalcazar served under Pedro Arias Davila during his campaign in Nicaragua in 1524. He then joined Pizarro on his expedition to Peru in 1531. In 1533 he set out on his own and conquered the Incas in Ecuador.

PANFILO DE NARVÁEZ

Under the command of Diego Velazquez, Narváez played an important part in the conquest of Cuba in 1511. In 1520 he was sent to Mexico to arrest Cortes for treason. Cortes took him prisoner and released him a year later. In 1527 he led a two-year expedition to Florida. Narváez drowned and only four of his men returned to Mexico.

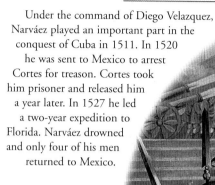

ALVAR NUNEZ CABEZA DE VACA

De Vaca joined the expedition to Florida under the leadership of Panfilo de Narváez. The expedition was a disaster and de Vaca was the only officer to survive. He and three other men eventually got back to Mexico. He was appointed the governor of the South American province of Rio de la Plata —what is now modern Paraguay. In 1541 he led an expedition from Santos in Brazil to Asuncion in Paraguay, a journey of over 1,000 miles.

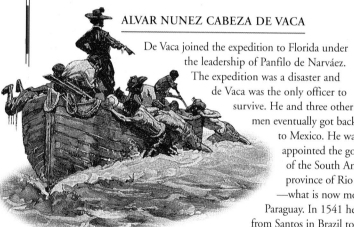

HERNANDO DE SOTO

De Soto is best known as the discoverer of the Mississippi River. He fought with Pizarro in the conquest of the Incas and was the first European to meet the Inca ruler, Atahualpa. With the backing of the Spanish king he led an expedition to Florida in 1539. He traveled through Florida, North and South Carolina, Alabama, and Mississippi. He discovered the Mississippi River in 1541.

Other Explorers of South America

80 CTS

FRANCISCO DE ORELLANA

ESPAÑA

1965   F. N. M. T.

Explorers went to America for many reasons. The stories of the vast wealth of South and Central America that found their way back to Spain must have persuaded many to try to make their fortunes in these newly discovered lands. This is one of the reasons why the Spaniards treated their new subjects so cruelly. Although the Spanish king and some priests tried to protect the people from being badly treated, they had little effect. Many of these explorers were interested only in getting rich as soon as possible and they were not concerned about those they had conquered. However, there were some who were driven by the belief that they were working for the glory of their god and country.

FRANCISCO DE ORELLANA

Orellana was the first person to explore the Amazon River. During an expedition into the interior of South America, Orellana found the Amazon and sailed along it for eight months until he reached the Atlantic. He then continued to Spain.

GONZALO JIMENEZ DE QUESADA

De Quesada was the Spanish conqueror of the Chibcha civilization of Columbia. In 1536 he set off to search for the legendary city of El Dorado. In 1537 he conquered the Chibchas and called the territory New Granada. While there he founded the town of Bogota.

BERNAL DIAZ DEL CASTILLO

Del Castillo was a Spanish soldier who kept a record of the conquest of the Aztecs by Cortes. Before joining Cortes, he had visited Panama and went to Yucatan in 1517 and 1518. In 1519 he accompanied Cortes to Mexico and he claimed to have fought in over 100 battles. He also fought in the conquest of El Salvador and Guatemala.

DID YOU KNOW?

Ancient civilizations We know very little about the lives of the Aztecs and Incas because the Spaniards destroyed everything that they found. Beautiful gold objects were melted down into gold bars. Books and drawings were burned as works of the devil. Bishop Diego de Landa of Yucatan came across some painted books and he later wrote: "*We found a great number of books in these letters of theirs, and because they had nothing but superstition and lies of the devil, we burned them all, which upset the Indians greatly, and caused them much pain.*" Most of the remains of Tenochtitlan were not discovered until the Mexicans began to build an underground railway system in Mexico City.

Sea journeys The main problem faced by sailors on long voyages was scurvy. This often-fatal disease is caused by a lack of vitamin C, which comes from fresh fruit and vegetables. Fresh food did not last long on the ships of the explorers. Sailors would become extremely tired and would start to bleed from the scalp and the gums. It was not until 1795, when the British gave fruit juice to all their sailors, that the problem began to disappear.

Trading vessels In the first part of the 16th century the carrack became the most popular European ship for trade, exploration, and warfare. Carracks became important symbols of national pride. In England Henry VIII had built the *Great Harry*, which was the largest carrack built up until that time. The French responded by building *La Grande Françoise,* which was even larger. Sadly, it was so large that it could not get out of the mouth of the harbor where it was built. By the end of the 16th century the carrack was being replaced by the galleon.

Ship's crew Most ships not only had ordinary sailors among the crew, but also carpenters, priests, cooks, doctors, gunners, blacksmiths, pilots, and boys as young as ten on board. Crew members normally came from many different countries and the captain sometimes had difficulty making them understand his instructions.

Aztec calendar The Aztec calendar stone worked in a very peculiar way. The calendar was made up of two wheels, one of top of the other. The small wheel had thirteen numbers carved or painted on it. The large wheel had the names of twenty days on it. These were the names of animals or plants. Numbers could then be lined up with a particular named day. Only the Aztec priests could read these and tell if a day was to be lucky or unlucky. For instance, 4 Dog was a good day to be born on. Anybody born on 2 Rabbit would not do so well. 1 Ocelot was seen as a good day for traveling.

First edition for the United States, its territories and dependencies, Canada and the Philippine Republic, published 1998 by Barron's Educational Series, Inc.
Original edition copyright © 1998 by Ticktock Publishing, Ltd.
U.S. edition copyright © 1998 by Barron's Educational Series, Inc.

All inquiries should be addressed to:
Barron's Educational Series, Inc.
250 Wireless Boulevard
Hauppauge, New York 11788
http://www.barronseduc.com
Library of Congress Catalog Card No. 97-77635
International Standard Book No. 0-7641-0531-0
Printed in Italy

Picture Credits: t=top, b=bottom, c=center, l=left, r=right
AKG (London); 1br, 1tl, 2br, 3b, 2/3t, 3tr, OFC, IFC & 4tl, 4bl, 5tl, OFC & 13br, OBC & 14tl, OFC & 14/15c, 15cr, 16br 16/17c, 17tr, 18/19c, 18br, 19bl, 19br, 22tl, 23tl, 22/23cb, 24tl, 24bl, 25tr, 28tl, 29tr, OBC & 28/29c. Ancient Art and Architecture; 1tl, OFC & 10/11ct, 12bl, 18l, OBC & 24r, 25bl, 25br, 32c. Ann Ronan @ Image Select; 2tl, 2/3c, 5tr, 4br, 7cr, 27tl. Archivo Fotográfico (Spain); OBC & 31tr. Asia; 6cb, OBC & 6bl, 8cl, 14bl, 19tr, 20ct, 23tr, 29br, 31br. Chris Fairclough/Image Select; 27tr. et Archive; OBC & 6tl, 11tr, 10bl, 15tr, 16c, 17br, 27br, 28bl. Giraudon; OFC, 8/9ct, 8/9c, 12/13c, 12tl, 22/23c, 24c. Image Select; 5bl, 7br, OBC & 6/7c, OFC & 10tl, 16tl, 20tl, OFC & 22bl. Index/Giraudon; 11br. Index (Spain); 8bl, 9br, 9c, 26/27c, 28/28cb, 30/31cb, 30cl. Institut Amatller d'art Hispanic; 31bl. Mary Evans; 30b. Nick Saunders/Barbara Heller @ Werner Forman Archive; 30tl. Pix; OBC & 6tr, 8br, 14bl, 20/21. Werner Forman Archive; 10br, 15br

Every effort has been made to trace the copyright holders and we apologize in advance for any unintentional omissions. We would be pleased to insert the appropriate acknowledgement in any subsequent edition of this publication.

BARRON'S